DISTORTED IMAGES OF GOD

Restoring Our Vision

8 STUDIES FOR INDIVIDUALS OR GROUPS

LifeGuide®
BIBLE STUDIES

DALE RYAN
AND JUANITA RYAN

IVP Connect

An imprint of InterVarsity Press
Downers Grove, Illinois

InterVarsity Press
P.O. Box 1400, Downers Grove, IL 60515-1426
ivpress.com
email@ivpress.com

InterVarsity Press® is the book-publishing division of InterVarsity Christian Fellowship/USA®, a movement of students and faculty active on campus at hundreds of universities, colleges and schools of nursing in the United States of America, and a member movement of the International Fellowship of Evangelical Students. For information about local and regional activities, visit intervarsity.org.

LifeGuide® is a registered trademark of InterVarsity Christian Fellowship.

Cover design: Cindy Kiple
Cover image: © Paul Knight / Trevillion Images

ISBN 978-0-8308-3145-6

Printed in the United States of America ∞

P	19	18	17	16	15	14	13	12	11	10
Y	28	27	26	25	24	23	22			

Contents

Getting the Most Out of
Distorted Images of God

What comes into our minds when we think about God is the most important thing about us. For this reason the gravest question before the Church is always God himself, and the most portentous fact about any man is not what he at a given time may say or do, but what he in his deep heart conceives God to be like.

A. W. TOZER, *The Knowledge of the Holy*

Most of us developed our concepts and feelings about our heavenly Father from our earthly mothers and fathers, and these feelings become intertwined and confused. But the guilty and contradictory feelings are not the voice of God. They are often the continuing voice of Mother or Dad or Brother or Sister, or something internalized that puts pressure on us. Most of our basic patterns for relating come from the patterns of the relationships of our family.

DAVID SEAMANDS, *Healing for Damaged Emotions*

According to A. W. Tozer, our images of God are critically important to our spiritual well-being. And, according to David Seamands, these images of God are formed to a large extent by experiences in our families.

None of us has lived in a perfect family. Many people have experienced parents or other family members as emotionally distant, unreliable, abusive, unrealistic in their expectations, inattentive and weak, or as ones who abandon or withhold. As a result, we may see the God of the Bible through distorted lenses—lenses that may interfere with our ability to talk honestly with God or to trust God. Even more, our distorted images of God may keep us from fully experiencing God's unfailing love for us.

Often our *images* of God influence us more powerfully than do our ideas or formal convictions *about* God, because images are rooted in powerful emotional experiences. Our images of God affect both how we feel about God and how we live in relationship to God. If we privately imagine God to be impossible to please, for example, we may spend our days feverishly slaving for the very One who invites us to rest. If we privately imagine God to be abusive we may spend our life hiding from the One who desires to carry us like a lamb close to the Shepherd's heart. If we imagine God to be emotionally distant we may live cut off emotionally from the God who promises us empathy, help and grace in our times of need.

Our images of God often lay buried deep within us. Because our distorted images often begin to form early in life, we may not even be aware of them. In *The Knowledge of the Holy,* Tozer explains the situation this way: "Our real idea of God may lie buried under the rubbish of conventional religious notions and may require an intelligent and vigorous search before it is finally unearthed and exposed for what it is. Only after an ordeal of painful self probing are we likely to discover what we actually believe about God."

Healing from our distorted images of God requires that we do the "vigorous search" to "unearth and expose" them, as Tozer suggests. At the same time, we also need to begin to read and reflect on imagery from Scripture about God, in ways that allow the good news of God's unfailing love for us to sink deep within our hearts and minds.

The following studies examine biblical texts that directly challenge common distorted images of God. Some of the questions will ask you to make observations about the text. Other questions will encourage you to interpret parts of the text, based on your observations, and to apply the truth of the passage to your life. And other questions will ask you to engage with the images of God that these Scriptures offer, either by putting yourself in the story as one of the characters or by reflecting on the text in a way that allows the imagery to speak to your mind, your heart and your life.

Because our distorted images of God are often rooted in painful emotional experiences, identifying them and pursuing healing can be an emotionally challenging experience. If you find this to be the case, we encourage you to seek out the support of a trusted friend, pastor, spiritual director or counselor. It is also important to remember that healing deeply from distorted images of God will likely mean healing slowly. None of us can change our distorted images of God simply by an act of our will, or by our own effort. What we can do is invite God to heal us and seek the support we need in the process. Our prayer is that these studies will be used by the Spirit to encourage you on your journey of identifying some of your distorted images of God and in gradually displacing these distortions with biblically accurate images of God.

May you experience God's healing presence as you come to see God more clearly.

Suggestions for Individual Study

1. As you begin each study, pray that God will speak to you through his Word.

2. Read the introduction to the study and respond to the personal reflection question or exercise. This is designed to help you focus on God and on the theme of the study.

3. Each study deals with a particular passage—so that you can delve into the author's meaning in that context. Read and reread the passage to be studied. The questions are written using the language of the New International Version, so you may wish to use that version of the Bible. The New Revised Standard Version is also recommended.

4. This is an inductive Bible study, designed to help you discover for yourself what Scripture is saying. The study includes three types of questions. Observation questions ask about the basic facts: who, what, when, where and how. Interpretation questions delve into the meaning of the passage. Application questions help you discover the implications of the text for growing in Christ. These three keys unlock the treasures of Scripture.

Write your answers to the questions in the spaces provided or in a personal journal. Writing can bring clarity and deeper understanding of yourself and of God's Word.

5. It might be good to have a Bible dictionary handy. Use it to look up any unfamiliar words, names or places.

6. Use the prayer suggestion to guide you in thanking God for what you have learned and to pray about the applications that have come to mind.

7. You may want to go on to the suggestion under "Now or Later," or you may want to use that idea for your next study.

Suggestions for Members of a Group Study

1. Come to the study prepared. Follow the suggestions for individual study mentioned above. You will find that careful preparation will greatly enrich your time spent in group discussion.

2. Be willing to participate in the discussion. The leader of your group will not be lecturing. Instead, he or she will be encouraging the members of the group to discuss what they have learned. The leader will be asking the questions that are found in this guide.

3. Stick to the topic being discussed. Your answers should be based on the verses which are the focus of the discussion and not on outside authorities such as commentaries or speakers. These studies focus on a particular passage of Scripture. Only rarely should you refer to other portions of the Bible. This allows for everyone to participate in in-depth study on equal ground.

4. Be sensitive to the other members of the group. Listen attentively when they describe what they have learned. You may be surprised by their insights! Each question assumes a variety of answers. Many questions do not have "right" answers, particularly questions that aim at meaning or application. Instead the questions push us to explore the passage more thoroughly.

When possible, link what you say to the comments of others. Also, be affirming whenever you can. This will encourage some of the more hesitant members of the group to participate.

5. Be careful not to dominate the discussion. We are sometimes so eager to express our thoughts that we leave too little opportunity for others to respond. By all means participate! But allow others to also.

6. Expect God to teach you through the passage being discussed and through the other members of the group. Pray that you will have an enjoyable and profitable time together, but also that as a result of the study you will find ways that you can take action individually and/or as a group.

7. Remember that anything said in the group is considered confidential and should not be discussed outside the group unless specific permission is given to do so.

8. If you are the group leader, you will find additional suggestions at the back of the guide.

1

The God of Impossible Expectations Versus the God of Compassion

Psalm 103:1-14

Children have a tremendous need for approval from their parents and other important adults in their lives. Unfortunately, some adults, for whatever reason, withhold encouraging words and speak only to correct and criticize. When children are unable to win the approval they seek, they may take in negative messages, not only about themselves but also about God.

The result may be that God is seen as one who is never pleased. God's standards seem impossible. God's expectations always appear to be beyond reach. The image of God that results from experiences of this kind is described clearly by David Seamands in *Healing for Damaged Emotions:*

> God . . . is seen as a figure on top of a tall ladder. [The person] says to himself, "I'm going to climb up to God now. I'm His child, and I want to please Him, more than I want anything else." So he starts climbing, rung by rung, working so hard, until his knuckles are bleeding and his shins are bruised. . . . He climbs and struggles, but when he gets up there, his God has gone up another three rungs.

. . . God is that little inner voice that always says, "That's not quite good enough."

In contrast to this distorted image, the God of the Bible is consistently presented as a gracious and merciful God who delights in each of us. The God of Scripture is a God who knows and accepts our limitations far better than we do ourselves.

GROUP DISCUSSION. Think of a little child you know and love— maybe a grandchild, a niece or nephew, your own child, or a child from your church. How will you respond to the child when he or she falls down in attempting to take his or her first steps? How will you respond when the child is hungry? How will you respond when watching the child play?

PERSONAL REFLECTION. What would it be like to live or work with someone who rarely seemed pleased with you?

Psalm 103 reveals a God who knows our limitations and needs and who responds to our human condition with forgiveness, healing, compassion, strengthening, guidance, patience and love. *Read Psalm 103:1-14.*

1. What words does the psalmist use as he calls himself to this act of giving thanks (vv. 1-2)?

2. What is involved in the act of giving thanks?

3. In your experience, what happens to us when we express gratitude or praise?

4. Make a list of all the things the psalmist gives thanks for in verses 1-8.

5. Which of these gifts from God are you especially grateful for at this time?

6. What do these verses reveal about God?

7. What does the psalmist say about God in verses 9-14?

8. Based on this psalm, how would you explain to someone else God's expectations of us?

9. How does the image of God presented in this text challenge the image of a god-of-impossible-expectations?

_____

10. How might this biblical image of God help you feel more accepted and loved by God?

_____

11. Responding with praise or thanksgiving is a way of taking in the gifts of love God offers us. Write your own response of gratitude to God who is full of compassion and love for you.

Invite God to heal any distortions you might have of God as a god-of-impossible-expectations. Pray for an increase in your ability to trust God's compassion for you.

Now or Later

Write a gratitude list each day this week, identifying specific gifts you are aware of receiving from God who is a God of compassion.

2

The Emotionally Distant God Versus the God of Empathy and Grace

Hebrews 4:14-16; 5:1-10

We are emotional beings who long for emotional connection with others. When others tune in to our emotions with understanding and empathy, we experience being seen and valued. A bond is formed, a relationship is created.

However, when significant others discount or judge our feelings, whether joy or fear or sadness, we can feel cut off and alone. We might even feel shame. The result is often emotional distance in the relationship.

When we suffer from such emotional distance with significant others—whether parents, pastors or friends—we may start to see God as unsympathetic and emotionally distant, cold and unapproachable. We may be left wondering, *How could God understand my problems? Why would God even care about what I feel?*

However, the image of an emotionally distant God is dramatically different from the image of Immanuel, "God with us." God came and lived with us, as one of us. God, in Jesus, experienced our temptations and struggles and feelings.

GROUP DISCUSSION. Think about a relationship in which you have experienced emotional closeness. What are the benefits to you of having someone know and care about you emotionally?

PERSONAL REFLECTION. What experiences in your life may have impacted your ability to see God as sympathetic and approachable?

Scripture teaches that God empathizes with us and offers us an intimacy that includes the emotional closeness for which we long. *Read Hebrews 4:14-16 and 5:1-10.*

1. What do you learn about the role of a priest in these verses?

2. According to these verses, what was it that allowed a high priest to "deal gently" with people?

3. From these verses, what qualifications does Jesus have to serve in this capacity?

4. What valuable roles might the high priest have played in the lives of the people?

---

5. Given these descriptions of Jesus' experience, what does it mean that Jesus can "sympathize with our weaknesses"?

---

6. Why is it important to know that Jesus can sympathize with our weaknesses?

---

7. According to this passage, how can we expect God to respond to us when we are in need?

---

8. How does this text's image of God-who-sympathizes-with-our-weakness compare or contrast with the image of a god-who-is-emotionally-distant?

9. Spend a few quiet minutes with God. Picture yourself approaching Jesus confidently. Picture Jesus understanding your feelings. Listen as he says to you, "Receive my mercy; here is grace for you in your time of need."

Describe your experience during this meditation.

---

10. What difference would it make to you as you face your current struggles to know that God deeply understands what you are going through and empathizes with you?

Take some time to share your needs and feelings with God-who-sympathizes-with-your-weaknesses.

Now or Later

Continue to identify your feelings this week and share them with the God who sympathizes with you. Keep a journal of the feelings you share with God and any sense you have of God providing you the help and compassion you need.

3

The Inattentive God
Versus the God Who
Knows Us Intimately

Psalm 139:1-18

"I just wish my parents would give me some attention! I feel so alone." These were the words of a fourteen-year-old girl who had been admitted to the hospital after a suicide attempt. She was angry and lonely and ready to give up on life because she did not experience her parents as interested in her.

Parents are busy people. Their lives are full of anxieties about work and money and relationships. They live with a great deal of stress. They work long hours. They are tired. Sometimes they are depressed. They may have learned from their own childhoods not to talk and not to feel. So they may not be very good at helping their children talk and feel, and can end up communicating a lack of interest in their children. Even if they do manage to show interest in their child's performance in athletics or in academics, they can still fail to communicate interest in the child as a person.

People who experienced their parents as inattentive often come to view God as inattentive as well. God may seem to be too busy with other matters to care or to listen or to even know that they exist. As a result, it may be very difficult for them to imagine that God could be intimately attentive to their daily joys and struggles of life.

The God found in the Bible, however, is intimately involved with us in every aspect of our lives. God is interested in what we need and think and feel and do, paying close, loving attention to us.

GROUP DISCUSSION. Think of experiences you have had with someone being lovingly attentive to you. What were those experiences like for you?

PERSONAL REFLECTION. Reflect on the thought that God is lovingly attentive to you at all times. What response do you have to this thought about God?

Psalm 139 reveals a Creator who knows us intimately—a God who is with us, watching over us, loving us all the days of our lives, in every place and every circumstance. *Read Psalm 139:1-18.*

1. Make a list of all the verbs used in this text to describe God's activities.

2. Now look over your list. What does all this active involvement in our lives communicate about God's character?

What does it reveal about God's abilities (especially in comparison to our human capabilities)?

---

3. What is the psalmist's response to God's attentiveness (vv. 6, 17-18)?

---

4. Looking again at your list of verbs, what is your response to these descriptions of God's active, loving involvement and attention in your life?

---

5. What is the significance of the imagery in verses 11-12?

---

6. Which of the descriptions of God's constant, attentive presence speaks the most to you at this time? Explain.

---

7. Paraphrase the stanza that the description you chose comes from.

What new insight did you gain?

8. How does this image of God-who-is-attentive contrast with the image of an inattentive god?

9. How might it affect you on a daily basis to trust that God pays loving attention to every detail of your life?

10. Write your own brief psalm of response to God based on what you've learned and experienced in this study. You might start with the words "Oh Lord, you know me, you see me, you are with me when . . ."

Express your gratitude to God-who-is-attentive for the ways God lovingly sees you and every detail of your life.

Now or Later

At the end of each day this week, review the day, asking God to bring to your awareness the many ways that God was lovingly attending to you throughout the day.

4

The Abusive God Versus the God Who Heals Us

Matthew 20:29-34

We all are created with a longing to love and a longing to be loved. We long for relationships marked by kindness, respect, empathy and affection.

Unfortunately, too many people experience harsh criticism instead of affection, and abusive punishment instead of kindness and respect from important people in their lives. Too many people have encounters with peers, pastors or family members that convince them that they are not lovable or valuable or capable. And too many people are the victims of violent actions that leave them terrified and violated.

Experiences of emotional, spiritual, physical or sexual abuse can shatter any image of a loving God. God may be seen instead as easily angered and demanding. People can end up living with a private fear that if they don't think and act just right, God will punish them.

But the God of the Bible is not an abusive bully. God is not easily angered. God does not yell hurtful words at us or stand ready to club us. The God found in Scripture is, rather, the father of compassion. The God of the Bible is the God who heals us.

GROUP DISCUSSION. If someone believes that God is abusive, what specific images might they have of such a God?

PERSONAL REFLECTION. What personal experiences might affect your ability to believe that God wants to heal you rather than hurt you?

The following story from the Gospel of Matthew is one of many stories of Jesus healing the sick, the lame and the blind. In Jesus we encounter the God who listens to us with compassion and responds to us by healing our wounds. *Read Matthew 20:29-34.*

1. What title would you give to this story?

2. When the blind men called to Jesus for mercy, "the crowd rebuked them and told them to be quiet." What kinds of things do you think the crowd might have said to these men?

3. Even beyond their words, what attitudes do you think the crowd might have had toward the blind men?

4. Compare Jesus' reaction to the men with the crowd's reaction. What did Jesus say and do in this passage?

_____

5. What do Jesus' words and actions suggest about his attitude toward the men?

_____

6. Jesus told his disciples that, having seen him, they had seen the Father (John 14:9-10). Given that Jesus came to show us the loving heart and face of God, what does Jesus' response to these men show us about God?

_____

7. In addition to receiving their sight, how were the lives of the two men changed as a result of their encounter with Jesus?

_____

8. How does the portrait of Jesus in this text challenge the image of an abusive God?

9. What experiences have you had of God's healing in your life?

10. How would it help you with your current struggles to know that God loves you and desires to heal you?

11. Reread this passage, putting yourself in the story as someone in the crowd. See the scene, and hear yourself and others responding to the blind men. Then hear and see Jesus' response. Make a brief note of your experience.

Now read the story again, this time putting yourself in the story as one of the blind men. Call out to Jesus for mercy. Hear the crowd's response to you. Take in Jesus' responses to you. Make a brief note of your experience.

Spend some time talking to God-who-heals about whatever healing you need today.

Now or Later

Read Matthew 15:29-39. Reread it slowly three times, sitting quietly for two to three minutes after each reading. Put yourself in the story each time as someone who was healed and fed by Jesus. Let yourself absorb this healing, compassionate encounter with Jesus. Write about your experience.

5

The Unreliable God Versus the God Who Is Trustworthy

Psalm 145:1-16

Many children conclude from observing the adults in their lives that people are unreliable. Adults sometimes make promises they do not keep. They sometimes get angry when there seems to be nothing to be angry about. They may be loving, attentive and kind at times and hostile, inattentive and unkind at other times. And these changes may take place without explanation and without an opportunity for clarification.

We all need love that's reliable and predictable in order to develop trust. When people whom we depend on are unreliable, we might feel confused and disappointed and, as a result, decide that we cannot count on others. We start to believe we can only count on ourselves.

When we have been repeatedly disappointed by parents or other significant people in our lives, we may, without even realizing it, come to see God as unreliable too—someone who cannot be trusted, who might be loving one day and unaccountably angry or distant the next. We may fear that we cannot really trust God's promises of grace and love and help.

The good news is that the image of an unreliable God stands in stark contrast to biblical images of God. The God of the Bible is the Faithful One, the Rock, the Fortress, the one who is "the same yesterday and today and forever," as the author of Hebrews put it (Hebrews 13:8). The God of Scripture is a God of unfailing faithfulness and love.

GROUP DISCUSSION. Think of a person whom you see as reliable or trustworthy. Describe the person and your relationship to him or her.

PERSONAL REFLECTION. Describe one or two experiences in your life that could have led you to conclude that people were either reliable or unreliable. What feelings do you have as you recall these events?

Psalm 145 is a psalm of praise to the God "whose kingdom is everlasting, whose dominion endures through all generations" and who "is faithful to all his promises and loving toward all he has made" (v. 13). *Read Psalm 145:1-16.*

1. What does the psalmist say that one generation will tell to the next (vv. 3-7)?

2. What does this pattern of one generation telling these truths about God to the next say about God's constancy, faithfulness and trustworthiness?

3. What does the psalmist say that he will do in response to God (vv. 1-7)?

What effect do you think these activities might have on him?

4. How else does the psalmist describe the Lord and his kingdom (vv. 8-13)?

5. In verses 13-16 the psalmist paints an even more tender picture of God. Paraphrase what he says here.

6. What image of God comes through to you most clearly from this psalm?

7. How do the images of God in this text challenge the image of an unreliable god?

8. How would your life change if you were to more fully trust and believe that God is gracious, compassionate, rich in love and good to all, faithful to all his promises and loving toward all he has made?

9. What are some of the specific ways and times that you have seen God's trustworthiness in your life?

10. In order to correct distorted images of God, we need to allow ourselves to be engaged by the biblical text. Read the following phrases from verses 13-16: "The LORD is faithful to all his promises and loving toward all he has made. The LORD upholds all those who fall and lifts up all who are bowed down. You open your hand and satisfy the desires of every living thing." Sit with these images for a few minutes. Then reread the phrases and sit with the images again for a few minutes.

Describe your thoughts and feelings during this meditation.

Spend some time talking to God-who-is-trustworthy, asking for a greater capacity to trust in God's unfailing love.

Now or Later

Ask God to heal you so that you can learn to rely on God's un-failing love more fully every day. Express thanks to God each day for the ways you see God's faithfulness and trustworthiness in your life. Keep a journal of your daily experiences of learn-ing to trust God's love for you and for others.

6

The God Who Abandons
Versus the God Who Pursues

Luke 15:1-7

Separation. Divorce. Death. Prolonged hospitalization of a parent. Mom's or Dad's endless hours at the bar. Or at work. Or at church. For a child, these are experiences of abandonment. One of their parents, to whom they look for their very survival, has left them.

Any type of abandonment is terribly traumatic for a child, in part because their perspective of reality is very limited. When they ask, "Why would my parent leave me?" the conclusion they arrive at is often, "It must have been my fault. If I had been better [or happier or nicer], my parent would not have left." A child who has been abandoned can therefore end up with feelings of anxiety and over-responsibility. Their sense of security may be destroyed. And they may harbor a deep fear that other people they love will leave too.

Out of this insecurity and fear grows an image of God as one who will also abandon. Because of this fear, a person may try very hard to please God, hoping that God will not leave. But the fear of abandonment by God may always be there.

GROUP DISCUSSION. Have you ever seen a child in a public place who has been separated from their parent(s)? What did you observe? What did you do?

PERSONAL REFLECTION. Describe a time when you felt alone or abandoned or forgotten. Describe a time when you felt remembered and loved.

The god-who-abandons is not the God of the Bible. Scripture presents us with God-who-will-never-leave-or-forsake-us and God-who-will-be-with-us-until-the-end. Moreover, when we are lost, God-the-Good-Shepherd will pursue us and will carry us home with great joy. *Read Luke 15:1-7.*

1. How does the tax collectors' and sinners' response to Jesus differ from that of the Pharisees and teachers of the law?

What is significant about this difference in responses?

2. Why do you think the Pharisees believe it is wrong for Jesus to "[welcome] sinners and [eat] with them"?

3. Put yourself in the place of one of the Pharisees or teachers of the law. You are highly educated, highly religious and highly respected. You believe Jesus is very wrong for eating with "sin-

ners." Privately you have tried very hard to please God, but you feel like you cannot do enough to keep God from judging you and abandoning you. How might you experience the story Jesus tells in this text?

4. Put yourself in the place of one of the "sinners" listening to this story. You cannot imagine that God could care about you. Because of your own choices or because of how you have been treated by others, you believe God has abandoned you. How might you experience this story?

5. What does this story tell us about how God sees us?

6. What does this story tell us about God?

7. How does the image of God that Jesus gives us in the story compare with your personal images of God?

8. How might the realization that God has taken the initiative to have a relationship with you help you to be more secure in that relationship?

9. Imagine for a few moments that you have gotten caught in a thicket. God notices that you are missing and sets out to find you. Imagine that when God finds you, God's face is full of joy; God's response to seeing you is delight that is rooted in love. Let God pick you up and carry you close. You are found. You are loved by your Maker, your Shepherd God. Sit with this image for a few minutes.

Describe your thoughts and feelings in response to this meditation.

---

10. What difference would it make to you in your current struggles to remember that God will never leave you but will always pursue you in love?

Spend some time thanking God for being God-who-seeks-you-and-rejoices-over-you.

Now or Later

Spend time each day this week with the images from Jesus' story. Reread the story slowly and sit with it for a few minutes, and then read it again. And again. Write about your experience as you do this each day.

7

The God Who Withholds
Versus the God Who Provides

As human babies, we all come into the world completely dependent. At birth and for many years thereafter, we need adults to provide food, clothing, shelter, safety, empathy, structure, guidance, affirmation, and a sense of belonging and of being valued and loved in order to survive and thrive. Without this kind of support, we will die, either physically, psychologically or spiritually. Our sense of ourself as valuable and our sense of others as trustworthy will be damaged. And our ability to trust in God-who-provides will be replaced with deeply rooted anxiety about whether or not God is prepared to care for us in the ways we need.

Jesus often spoke about anxiety and provision. He understood that deficits in care can lead to deep, sometimes disabling, fears that we are not valued, that we are not loved, that we are on our own to provide for ourselves. He also understood that these anxieties are connected to our anxieties about God. So he spoke directly to our worst fears, often talking about God as the One who feeds the birds, nourishes the flowers and pours out good gifts from a heart of unfailing love.

GROUP DISCUSSION. What experiences might help a child know that they are loved and valued?

PERSONAL REFLECTION. What fears are you aware of about God's desire to provide good things for you?

In the following texts from Matthew's Gospel, Jesus addresses our anxieties. Will God provide for us? Does God value us enough to care about our needs? Yes, Jesus answers. Yes. God values us even more than the lilies of the field or the birds of the air whom God sustains. God loves us more than the most loving human parent loves his or her own child. *Read Matthew 6:25-34 and 7:7-11.*

1. In Matthew 6:25-32 Jesus acknowledges that we worry about many things in life. What are the specific worries that Jesus names?

2. What threat does the lack of these things hold for us?

3. How do your worries about these things get expressed?

4. What change of perspective is Jesus offering to his listeners as he speaks about the birds and the lilies of the field?

5. In verse 26 Jesus talks about our value to God. Why is it sometimes—or even often—hard to believe we are deeply valued by God?

6. What practices might help you come to believe more deeply that you are incredibly valuable to God?

7. What does Jesus mean by his call to "seek first [God's] kingdom and his righteousness"?

8. In Matthew 7:7-11 Jesus continues the conversation about God's desire to provide for us. What does Jesus say about God's desire to give us good gifts?

9. How does the image of God that Jesus offers challenge the image of a god-who-withholds-good-things?

10. What difference might it make in your life to trust in God's goodness and desire to provide for your needs?

---

11. Even though God gives gifts in abundance without our asking, Jesus suggests that our part in receiving God's good gifts is in asking, seeking and knocking. Why might these be important activities for us?

---

12. In a time of quiet, open your hands as a symbol of openness to God's goodness. Ask God to help you let go of your worries. Turn each worry over to God's loving care. As you continue to sit with hands open in prayer, ask God to increase your capacity to trust in God's desire to provide all you need. With hands open, receive God's care for you, God's dearly loved child.

Share with God-who-provides whatever needs and concerns you have today.

Now or Later

Spend time in prayer at the beginning of each day with open hands, letting go of worry, entrusting yourself to God's loving care. At the end of each day, write about your observations of the ways God cared for you throughout the day.

8

The God Who Is Weak Versus the God Who Is All-Powerful

Luke 8:22-56

Children look to their parents for guidance and security. They need their parents to be strong and capable. But sometimes parents are overwhelmed or ill or depressed. Sometimes parents are passive. Sometimes they're frightened. Much of life is beyond a parent's control. Illness, accidents and tragedies happen. All these signs of human weakness can be deeply unsettling for children.

But God, our true Parent, is all-powerful. God's power is the power that created and continues to create. It is the power that sustains and contains and heals and blesses and provides. God's power is the power of love—a love that flows constantly from the heart of God into our lives, into our world.

In spite of evidence everywhere in creation of God's creative, sustaining power, many of us come to believe that God is weak in some way, and that God needs us to take over and be in charge. We may literally try to "play god" in our own lives and in the lives of others. Jesus came to show us the hands and face and power of the love of God. He calmed the storm, drove out demons, healed the sick and restored life to a child. The power of love to bless and release and redeem is a Power to whom we can entrust our lives.

GROUP DISCUSSION. When you think of God's power, what images or stories come to mind?

PERSONAL REFLECTION. What experiences in your past might make it difficult for you to trust the power of God's love?

The God of the Bible is the Creator and Sustainer of all things whose active, powerful love was demonstrated to us in Jesus. *Read Luke 8:22-56.*

1. What headline would you give to each of these four stories from Jesus' ministry?

2. In the first story, after Jesus calms the storm, the disciples ask each other, "Who is this?" What do you imagine they were saying to each other in answer to this question?

3. In the second story, the people of the region of the Garasenes, where Jesus healed the demon-possessed man, ask Jesus to leave the area because they are afraid. What do you think caused them to feel afraid?

4. In the third story, the woman who is healed had been suffering for twelve years, and no one was able to help her. What do you imagine she was thinking and feeling as she reached out to Jesus?

What do you imagine she experienced as she returned home that day?

5. In the fourth story, Jairus and his wife witness Jesus restore a child they believed to be dead. The text says they "were astonished." What might they have come to believe about Jesus and about God the Father that day?

6. Read through this passage again slowly, pausing briefly after each of the four stories. Put yourself in the place of one of the disciples. Watch Jesus calm the raging storm. Watch him free the demon-possessed man from terrible suffering. Listen as he blesses the bleeding woman for her faith—even though, according to the law, her touch would have made him unclean—and confirms both her healing and his love for her. Watch as he goes to the little girl whose anguished parents believe she is dead; listen as he takes the child by the hand and speaks to her. Let yourself take it all in as much as you can.

What was your experience as you placed yourself in these stories?

What new details did you notice?

7. What overall response do you have to these stories of God's work?

8. Which story speaks to you the most, and why?

9. What do these four stories show us about God?

10. How does this view of God challenge perceptions of a god-who-is-weak?

11. How might it change your life to trust that God's love is powerful enough and tender enough to calm storms, heal the sick and possessed, and raise the dead?

Talk with God about whatever powerful calming, freeing, healing or restoring you need.

Now or Later

Each day this week, reread the story from this text that spoke to you the most. Continue to let the story of God's powerful love speak to you. Write a prayer, inviting God to show you the power of God's love in tangible ways in your own life.

Leader's Notes

Leading a Bible discussion can be an enjoyable and rewarding experience. But it can also be *scary*—especially if you've never done it before. If this is your feeling, you're in good company. When God asked Moses to lead the Israelites out of Egypt, he replied, "O Lord, please send someone else to do it!" (Ex 4:13). It was the same with Solomon, Jeremiah and Timothy, but God helped these people in spite of their weaknesses, and he will help you as well.

You don't need to be an expert on the Bible or a trained teacher to lead a Bible discussion. The idea behind these inductive studies is that the leader guides group members to discover for themselves what the Bible has to say. This method of learning will allow group members to remember much more of what is said than a lecture would.

These studies are designed to be led easily. As a matter of fact, the flow of questions through the passage from observation to interpretation to application is so natural that you may feel that the studies lead themselves. This study guide is also flexible. You can use it with a variety of groups—student, professional, neighborhood or church groups. Each study takes forty-five to sixty minutes in a group setting.

There are some important facts to know about group dynamics and encouraging discussion. The suggestions listed below should enable you to effectively and enjoyably fulfill your role as leader.

Preparing for the Study

1. Ask God to help you understand and apply the passage in your

own life. Unless this happens, you will not be prepared to lead others. Pray too for the various members of the group. Ask God to open your hearts to the message of his Word and motivate you to action.

2. Read the introduction to the entire guide to get an overview of the entire book and the issues which will be explored.

3. As you begin each study, read and reread the assigned Bible passage to familiarize yourself with it.

4. This study guide is based on the New International Version of the Bible. It will help you and the group if you use this translation as the basis for your study and discussion.

5. Carefully work through each question in the study. Spend time in meditation and reflection as you consider how to respond.

6. Write your thoughts and responses in the space provided in the study guide. This will help you to express your understanding of the passage clearly.

7. It might help to have a Bible dictionary handy. Use it to look up any unfamiliar words, names or places. (For additional help on how to study a passage, see chapter five of *How to Lead a LifeGuide Bible Study,* InterVarsity Press.)

8. Consider how you can apply the Scripture to your life. Remember that the group will follow your lead in responding to the studies. They will not go any deeper than you do.

9. Once you have finished your own study of the passage, familiarize yourself with the leader's notes for the study you are leading. These are designed to help you in several ways. First, they tell you the purpose the study guide author had in mind when writing the study. Take time to think through how the study questions work together to accomplish that purpose. Second, the notes provide you with additional background information or suggestions on group dynamics for various questions. This information can be useful when people have difficulty understanding or answering a question. Third, the leader's notes can alert you to potential problems you may encounter during the study.

10. If you wish to remind yourself of anything mentioned in the leader's notes, make a note to yourself below that question in the study.

Leading the Study

1. Begin the study on time. Open with prayer, asking God to help the group to understand and apply the passage.

2. Be sure that everyone in your group has a study guide. Encourage the group to prepare beforehand for each discussion by reading the introduction to the guide and by working through the questions in the study.

3. At the beginning of your first time together, explain that these studies are meant to be discussions, not lectures. Encourage the members of the group to participate. However, do not put pressure on those who may be hesitant to speak during the first few sessions. You may want to suggest the following guidelines to your group.

☐ Stick to the topic being discussed.

☐ Your responses should be based on the verses which are the focus of the discussion and not on outside authorities such as commentaries or speakers.

☐ These studies focus on a particular passage of Scripture. Only rarely should you refer to other portions of the Bible. This allows for everyone to participate in in-depth study on equal ground.

☐ Anything said in the group is considered confidential and will not be discussed outside the group unless specific permission is given to do so.

☐ We will listen attentively to each other and provide time for each person present to talk.

☐ We will pray for each other.

4. Have a group member read the introduction at the beginning of the discussion.

5. Every session begins with a group discussion question. The question or activity is meant to be used before the passage is read. The question introduces the theme of the study and encourages group members to begin to open up. Encourage as many members as possible to participate, and be ready to get the discussion going with your own response.

This section is designed to reveal where our thoughts or feelings need to be transformed by Scripture. That is why it is especially important not to read the passage before the discussion question is asked. The passage will tend to color the honest reactions people would otherwise give because they are, of course, supposed to think the way the Bible does.

You may want to supplement the group discussion question with an icebreaker to help people to get comfortable. See the community section of *Small Group Idea Book* for more ideas.

You also might want to use the personal reflection question with your group. Either allow a time of silence for people to respond individually or discuss it together.

6. Have a group member (or members if the passage is long) read aloud the passage to be studied. Then give people several minutes to read the passage again silently so that they can take it all in.

7. Question 1 will generally be an overview question designed to briefly survey the passage. Encourage the group to look at the whole passage, but try to avoid getting sidetracked by questions or issues that will be addressed later in the study.

8. As you ask the questions, keep in mind that they are designed to be used just as they are written. You may simply read them aloud. Or you may prefer to express them in your own words.

There may be times when it is appropriate to deviate from the study guide. For example, a question may have already been answered. If so, move on to the next question. Or someone may raise an important question not covered in the guide. Take time to discuss it, but try to keep the group from going off on tangents.

9. Avoid answering your own questions. If necessary, repeat or rephrase them until they are clearly understood. Or point out something you read in the leader's notes to clarify the context or meaning. An eager group quickly becomes passive and silent if they think the leader will do most of the talking.

10. Don't be afraid of silence. People may need time to think about the question before formulating their answers.

11. Don't be content with just one answer. Ask, "What do the rest of you think?" or "Anything else?" until several people have given answers to the question.

12. Acknowledge all contributions. Try to be affirming whenever possible. Never reject an answer. If it is clearly off-base, ask, "Which

verse led you to that conclusion?" or again, "What do the rest of you think?"

13. Don't expect every answer to be addressed to you, even though this will probably happen at first. As group members become more at ease, they will begin to truly interact with each other. This is one sign of healthy discussion.

14. Don't be afraid of controversy. It can be very stimulating. If you don't resolve an issue completely, don't be frustrated. Move on and keep it in mind for later. A subsequent study may solve the problem.

15. Periodically summarize what the group has said about the passage. This helps to draw together the various ideas mentioned and gives continuity to the study. But don't preach.

16. At the end of the Bible discussion you may want to allow group members a time of quiet to work on an idea under "Now or Later." Then discuss what you experienced. Or you may want to encourage group members to work on these ideas between meetings. Give an opportunity during the session for people to talk about what they are learning.

17. Conclude your time together with conversational prayer, adapting the prayer suggestion at the end of the study to your group. Ask for God's help in following through on the commitments you've made.

18. End on time.

Many more suggestions and helps are found in *How to Lead a LifeGuide Bible Study.*

Components of Small Groups
A healthy small group should do more than study the Bible. There are four components to consider as you structure your time together.

Nurture. Small groups help us to grow in our knowledge and love of God. Bible study is the key to making this happen and is the foundation of your small group.

Community. Small groups are a great place to develop deep friendships with other Christians. Allow time for informal interaction before and after each study. Plan activities and games that will help you get to know each other. Spend time having fun together going on a picnic or cooking dinner together.

Worship and prayer. Your study will be enhanced by spending time praising God together in prayer or song. Pray for each other's needs and keep track of how God is answering prayer in your group. Ask God to help you to apply what you are learning in your study.

Outreach. Reaching out to others can be a practical way of applying what you are learning, and it will keep your group from becoming self-focused. Host a series of evangelistic discussions for your friends or neighbors. Clean up the yard of an elderly friend. Serve at a soup kitchen together, or spend a day working on a Habitat house.

Many more suggestions and helps in each of these areas are found in *Small Group Idea Book.* Information on building a small group can be found in *Small Group Leaders' Handbook* and *The Big Book on Small Groups* (both from InterVarsity Press). Reading through one of these books would be worth your time.

Study 1. The God of Impossible Expectations Versus the God of Compassion. Psalm 103:1-14.

Purpose: To let go of distortions about God as someone who has impossible expectations, and to grow in our ability to receive God's active love and compassion for us.

Preparation note. You may want to bring paper and pencils for question eleven.

Question 1. The psalmist calls on his "soul" and "all his inmost being" to praise God, and to "forget not" all of God's good gifts to him. This is not an act of worship as mere performance. It is an act of worship that arises from the depths of the psalmist's heart, mind and spirit. It is a response of deep gratitude and love for who God is and for God's active involvement in his life.

Question 2. Expressing gratitude involves (1) noticing the gifts we are being given, (2) acknowledging the gifts and the giver of those gifts, (3) letting ourselves embrace and be embraced by the loving kindness and goodness that the gifts represent, (4) responding with open-hearted love to the love being shown to us, and (5) expressing our joy as we receive the gifts and the love.

Question 3. When we express our gratitude or praise to God, we open our heart and mind and spirit to take in the loving kindness and compassion of God. Expressing gratitude or praise allows us to receive more fully the reality that we are loved with God's unfailing love.

Question 4. Allow as much time as needed to identify the many compassionate activities of God that are the focus of the psalmist's gratitude.

Question 5. Guide group members to relate personally to the activities that the psalmist attributes to God. How have they experienced God's active care and compassion in their own lives?

Question 7. Encourage the group to take time to reflect on and paraphrase the statements about God in these verses.

Question 8. This psalm tells us that God "remembers that we are dust." In our world, dust is of no value. It is one of the things you try to get rid of when you clean house. But the use of the word *dust* in this text does not imply this kind of worthlessness. Rather the text is suggesting that God, who made us, knows our limits and our needs. God knows we need forgiveness, healing, rescuing, strengthening and the compassion of a father's tender heart toward his children. God actively offers us all of these good gifts not because we are worthless dust, but because we are precious children.

Question 9. The god-of-impossible-expectations does not understand that people have limits. But the God of Scripture recognizes that we are limited creatures; God "remembers that we are dust." The god-of-impossible-expectations may be full of anger when we fall short of perfection. But the God of the Bible is "slow to anger, abounding in love" —a love that is "as high as the heavens are above the earth." The god-of-impossible-expectations may be intolerant of us when we grow weary. But the God of Scripture renews our strength "like the eagle's." The god-of-impossible-expectations extends no grace, no mercy, no compassion. But the God of Scripture is full of compassion, mercy, forgiveness and healing love for us.

Many people think that God expects perfection. They believe that God expects them to try harder and harder to do better and better. Perfectionism, however, results in resentment and vicious, graceless self-condemnation. According to David Seamands, perfectionism is "the most disturbing emotional problem among evangelical Christians" (*Healing for Damaged Emotions* [Wheaton, Ill.: Victor, 1984], p.

79). Healing from perfectionism is not easy. It can take a long time to let go of impossible expectations and to internalize God's compassion. But it is a healing work that God desires to do in all of us.

Question 10. It can be freeing to know that we are known by God fully, with all our limitations and need. God's response to us—even when our limitations, our dust-ness, is in clear view—is tender compassion. This text offers us powerful truths about God's active, healing compassion for us.

Question 11. Allow time for group members to share their words of praise and gratitude to the God of compassion.

Study 2. The Emotionally Distant God Versus the God of Empathy and Grace. Hebrews 4:14-16; 5:1-10.

Purpose: To realize that God sympathizes with us.

Question 1. Unlike for the original recipients of this text, the image of a "great high priest" is culturally foreign to us. The author of the letter to the Hebrews tells us in 5:1 that the high priest's function was "to represent [the people] in matters related to God" and "to offer gifts and sacrifices for sins."

Question 2. The text tells us that religious leaders, the high priests, were just as subject to weakness as the people they represented before God. It was that shared awareness of need that created a sense of empathy and gentleness in the high priest toward the people.

Question 3. Verses 4:14-16 describe Jesus' access to God and his emotional availability to us. He has "gone through the heavens." He can "sympathize with our weaknesses." He "has been tempted in every way" that we have but was "without sin." In addition, verses 5:4-6 tell us that Jesus was chosen by God to be the high priest, just as all high priests were called by God.

Question 5. Sympathy is a complex interpersonal exchange. Here is how David Seamands describes Jesus' sympathy: "If He merely understood the *fact* of our infirmities, that would be good enough. But I've got better news for you. He even understands the *feeling* of our infirmities—not just the cripplings, not just the weaknesses, not just the emotional hang-ups and the inner conflicts, but the pain that comes from them. He understands the frustration, the anxiety, the depression, the hurts, the feelings of abandonment and loneliness and isolation and rejection. He who is touched with the feeling of our infirmities experiences the whole ghastly gamut of emotions which goes along with our weaknesses and our cripplings" (*Healing for Damaged Emotions*, pp. 39-40).

Question 6. Jesus' ability to sympathize with our weakness is an enormous gift of grace. Because of his personal understanding of our weaknesses—his willingness to come to earth and experience suffering and temptation as we do—we can know that his compassion is real and true. He offers us true emotional closeness, a tender intimacy, a compassion with depth and power—a compassion that can comfort and heal us.

Question 7. Because of Jesus' ability to sympathize with us, we can "approach the throne of grace with confidence." We can go to God with a sense of trust that we will be received with a love that is both tender and powerful. We can turn to God with confidence that we will not be dismissed. There will be no emotional distance. There will be no shame for what we are going through. We can be confident that we will be embraced with empathy that is deeply rooted in shared experience.

Question 8. Many people believe—at least in theory—that God is emotionally close and tenderhearted. But our many experiences in shame-based relationships can make it difficult for this belief to have any impact on our lives. God's personal attentiveness to our emotions and empathic response to our struggles may be a very stark contrast to the shaming, distancing and disappointment that we have come to expect.

Question 9. Because the wounds that gave birth to our distorted images are often lodged deep within us, healing from these distortions will require that we engage our intellects, our emotions, our wills and our imaginations. This activity is an opportunity to begin an encounter between our distorted images of God and the images of God offered in Scripture. We encourage you to ask God for help in trusting God to meet people in the quiet moments of meditation that you provide. Read the instructions aloud slowly. In a brief prayer, invite God's Spirit to speak the healing truth of God's empathy and grace to each person's heart and mind. Then read the text

"Receive my mercy; here is grace for you in your time of need"; repeat this three or four times, with a minute pause between each repetition. Give group members three or four minutes to continue to sit with these words from Scripture and with the still small voice of God's Spirit. When the time of meditation is over, give people a chance to write and talk about what they experienced in this time.

Study 3: The Inattentive God Versus the God Who Knows Us Intimately. Psalm 139:1-18.
Purpose: To challenge the distortion of the disinterested god and to see instead the God who knows us and who pays attention to us personally and intimately.
Preparation note. You will need to have paper and pencils or pens on hand for people to use in answering question ten.
Question 1. The verbs of this psalm are suggestive of God's ongoing activity in our lives. The psalmist says God searches us, knows us, perceives our thoughts, discerns our comings and goings, hems us in, lays a hand on us, guides us, holds us fast, has created our inmost being, has knit us together, sees us, ordains our days.
Question 2. Encourage group members to explore the significance of God's intimate attentiveness to us—in every moment and every activity of our lives, in every conceivable place we might be.
Question 3. It is clear that for the psalmist, God's intimate, personal attention is very good news. In verse 6 he says this knowledge is "too wonderful" and "too lofty." It is such good news that it is hard to believe, hard to take in. In verses 17 and 18 he describes God's attention to him (God's thoughts toward him) as precious, vast and beyond number.
Question 4. People who privately fear that God is punitive may have difficulty absorbing the reality of God's care described in this psalm. Others—those who privately fear that God is disinterested in them, for example—may have a hard time taking in the reality of such intimate, personal attention. Encourage the group to explore their personal responses (which may be mixed) to this text.
Question 5. The poetic imagery in verses 11 and 12 explores the thought that not even darkness separates us from God's attentive care for us.

God sees and knows us and is with us always. The darkness often represents places of great fear or distress, places where we cannot see our way, places where we feel lost and alone. But God does not become distant or disengaged or disinterested in us in these times or places.

Question 8. The contrast between the god-who-is-disinterested and the image of God as intimately, personally attentive to us could not be more stark. In this psalm we are told that we are deeply known, deeply valued, continually watched over, guided and held securely from our first moments of life through each and every day.

Question 10. Invite group members to share what they have written with the group. Thank each one who shares.

**Study 4: The Abusive God Versus the God Who Heals Us.
Matthew 20:29-34.**
Purpose: To come to see and know God as a God who sees us, loves us and heals us.

Preparation note. You may want to have paper and pencils on hand for question eleven.

Question 1. Welcome all suggestions for giving a title to this story. The purpose of this question is to help group members look at the various aspects of the story and to attempt to capture what they see as its essence. Titles might reflect the crowd's response, the blind men's experience, or Jesus' act of compassion and healing.

Question 2. Encourage the group to engage their imaginations with the text. The blind men are beggars. They are probably homeless. They are disabled. The crowd may have told them not only to "be quiet," as the text suggests, but also to not bother Jesus, to stop being a problem, that Jesus had better things to do than to stop and talk with them.

Question 3. It is clear that the crowd did not value these two men. They saw the blind men as "less than." The men had no money. They were destitute. They seemingly had nothing to offer. It is also very possible that the crowd believed that the two men were blind because God had punished them for some sin they had committed. As a result, the crowd may have felt spiritually justified in their devaluing of these men, and may have assumed that they were seeing these men as God saw them.

Question 4. Jesus treated the two men in ways that shattered all the prejudices and judgments of the crowd. He didn't respond to them as "less than." He didn't treat them as if they were objects of God's punishment. Rather, Jesus treated the two men with dignity and respect. He was not blinded, as the crowd was, to their value and worth. Jesus saw them as God sees us all—through eyes of love, eyes that valued them. Moreover, Jesus felt what they were feeling with them and then responded with his heart and hands. His response was intimate and personal; it was a response of love.

Jesus' behaviors make this all clear. He stopped to be with them. Jesus did not hurry past them to the next important thing he had to do. They were what was important. He also inquired about what they needed and wanted. He listened to them with compassion. And then he touched them and healed them.

Question 6. The entire encounter between Jesus and these two men is recorded in just a few short verses, but Matthew's brief record captures the active, healing love of God that is personal, intimate and powerful. Jesus showed us God's perspective on who we are. Jesus showed us our worth, our value, in God's eyes.

Question 7. The men received a life-transforming gift. They were seen, they were valued, they were loved. And because of that, they followed Jesus.

Question 8. We see in the crowd what abuse can look like. Because the crowd was spiritually blind to the value of these men, they judged them, dismissed them, silenced them, marginalized them and devalued them. Abuse always involves the inability to see and to treat another person as valuable; it always involves treating another person as "less than." It is a form of spiritual blindness. This is the core of all abuse.

The contrast between the crowd and Jesus is remarkable. We may expect God to respond to us like the crowd responded to these two men. We may expect God to see us through eyes of judgment. We may expect God to dismiss us, silence us and devalue us. But that is not the God Jesus revealed to us. God is a healing God, and he heals us with powerful, tender love that values us beyond our ability to grasp. We are seen, we are known, we are valued, we are loved by our Maker.

Question 11. Because the healing of distorted images must take place near the core of our persons, we must engage our intellects, our emotions, our wills and our imaginations. This activity provides an opportunity for our distorted images of God to come up against the images of God in Scripture. We encourage you to invite God to deepen your trust that God will meet people in the quiet moments of meditation that you provide. In a brief prayer, invite God's Spirit to speak the healing truth of God's healing love to each person's heart and mind.

Then read the text, inviting group members to put themselves in the scene as one of the crowd. What is it like to be part of the crowd? Give the group two or three minutes to sit with this scene from Scripture and with the still small voice of God's Spirit.

Then reread the text, this time inviting group members to put themselves in the scene as one of the blind men. What is it like to be the "needy person" in front of a crowd? What is it like to be seen and loved and touched by Jesus? Again, give the group two or three minutes to sit with this scene from Scripture and with the still small voice of the Spirit.

When the time of meditation is over, give people a chance to write and talk about what they experienced during the exercise.

Study 5. The Unreliable God Versus the God Who Is Trustworthy. Psalm 145:1-16.

Purpose: To deepen our trust in God's faithfulness.

Question 1. The psalmist says that one generation will tell the next about God's mighty acts and speak of God's glorious splendor. They will tell of the power of God's awesome works. They will celebrate God's abundant goodness and sing with joy of God's righteousness.

Question 2. The thought of one generation telling the next about God's might, splendor and goodness is based on the assumption that God remains the same from one generation to the next. God acts powerfully in goodness and righteousness now and always. God is faithful. God is sure. God is trustworthy.

Question 3. The psalmist says that he will exalt and praise God every day, meditate on God's wonderful works and proclaim God's great deeds.

Meditating and proclaiming are an interesting mix of responses.

Meditation involves a focused, quiet reflection on something. It allows a person to take in, turn over, spend time with the object of meditation. Proclaiming, on the other hand, involves speaking, sharing, telling others about something. It is an outward acknowledgment of something. Different as they are, however, both activities do allow something to be more fully seen and known.

Question 4. The psalmist describes God as gracious, compassionate, slow to anger, rich in love, good to all, mighty, and king of a glorious, everlasting kingdom.

Question 5. Encourage group members to reflect on these images for a few minutes before paraphrasing these verses.

Question 6. The images of God in this psalm are that God is our Creator, our Sustainer, our Everlasting King who loves all and provides for all. This is a Creator who attends to all, who can be relied on to respond to our needs, and who takes special care with those who fall and those who are bowed down. This is a God who is "faithful to all his promises" (v. 13)—a central theme of both the Old and New Testaments.

Question 10. As with earlier times of meditation, invite God's Spirit to speak to each person through the reading of these words from Scripture.

Study 6. The God Who Abandons Versus the God Who Pursues. Luke 15:1-7.

Purpose: To see God as a God who pursues us.

Question 1. When Luke wrote his Gospel, he placed Jesus' words "He who has ears to hear, let him hear" (14:35) right before this parable. The two different responses to Jesus in Luke 15:1-7 illustrate for us what it looks like to truly hear Jesus' words. The people who were identified as tax collectors and "sinners" responded by actively listening to Jesus in order to hear what he had to say. The Pharisees (the religious leaders of the day), on the other hand, responded by muttering.

The "sinners" gathered around Jesus with the intention of listening to him. They were eager, teachable and aware of their need for the wisdom and guidance Jesus had to offer. They wanted to know what Jesus had to say about God and about them.

The Pharisees, on the other hand, were more defensive. They had worked hard to "get it all right," spending years trying to behave according to the strictest interpretation of the law and to believe according to the dogma of the day. They were not very teachable. Rather, they were closed to what Jesus had to say and to who Jesus was.

Question 2. The Pharisees would have been deeply disturbed by Jesus' friendship with tax collectors and "sinners" because they would have seen sharing a meal with "sinners" as an act of approval and acceptance—and as something that made a person "unclean." Any association with "sinners" was unacceptable to their way of thinking. This obviously meant that they did not see themselves as needy. The Pharisees most likely believed in a demanding, harsh god who judged and condemned people who were not keeping the law. They saw themselves as better than people who were less religious than they were. If Jesus was to be accepted by them as a prophet or a rabbi, he would have needed to separate himself from people who were "sinners." Instead, Jesus challenged all of their assumptions. He demonstrated a love for and valuing of all humans, without exception. And he taught that the love and acceptance he demonstrated for all people was a direct reflection of the Father whose will he had come to do.

Question 3. Encourage group members to place themselves in the narrative as one of these men. They had worked hard to earn God's favor. They felt they deserved to be seen as "better than" others, especially better than "sinners." Didn't they deserve some special status or preference? Jesus' story paints a very different image of who God is and who we all are. For some people this must have been deeply unsettling. But for others, it may have felt like very good news—news about a God who pursues us with love.

Question 4. For the tax collectors and "sinners," this story was probably deeply moving. They would have more easily seen themselves as the lost lamb, and were probably trying to imagine God, the Good Shepherd, pursuing them in love, experiencing joy upon finding them, speaking kindly to them, carrying them home. For some, the grace, love and tenderness of this story may have been life-changing.

Question 5. It suggests that God sees us in our true state of needing help and care, that God highly values us and delights in us, and that God thinks we are worth pursuing when we lose our way.

Question 6. The text shows us that God wants to have a relationship with us, that God is aware of our wanderings and loves to help us, that God pursues us, and that God greets us with joy and delight—rather than with shame or anger.

Question 9. Invite the Spirit to speak to each heart and mind in this time of meditation. Read this paragraph through once, allowing two minutes of silence after the reading. Then reread the paragraph again, again allowing two minutes of silent reflection. You may want to give the group a minute or two to write about their experience before inviting people to share.

Study 7. The God Who Withholds Versus the God Who Provides. Matthew 6:25-34; 7:7-11.

Purpose: To increase our trust in the God who provides.

Question 1. Jesus specifically mentioned our anxieties about not having food, drink or clothes to wear. And his use of the future tense shows that he knows that even if we have food and drink and clothes today, we worry about whether we will have enough tomorrow, or next week, or in a few years.

Question 2. Jesus was addressing our fundamental anxieties in life. The threat we feel is at the level of our survival. Some people do, of course, struggle daily to figure out where their next meal is coming from, but Jesus was addressing all of us, whether or not that's our specific situation. We all experience anxieties related to survival and security.

Question 3. Give the group time to reflect on the anxieties they experience. How do those fears and anxieties impact their thoughts and choices? How do people try to cope with their anxieties?

Group members may identify a variety of ways in which anxiety manifests itself. Sometimes our minds race with anxiety. Sometimes there are sleepless nights. Sometimes we lose ourselves in distractions of various kinds in an attempt to ease the anxiety. Often we try to control things that are out of our control. This strategy, doomed to fail, will eventually leave us tired, depressed and resentful. If we're trying to correct or control other people, in particular, it can also do significant harm to our relationships.

Question 4. Jesus is addressing some of the most basic questions in life. He is engaging his audience with the question "What is life all about?" He is also challenging them to consider what they can control and what they cannot control—reminding them that much of life, and most of the things we worry about are out of our control. But most importantly, Jesus is saying that the God who made us will provide for us. Jesus is saying that God knows all our needs and will meet our needs. Jesus is proclaiming that God sees us, loves us, values us and can be trusted with our needs.

Question 5. Trusting God's goodness and love turns out to be a difficult thing to do. All of us have had experiences with humans that have left us with reasons not to trust. And often, those experiences get blamed on God or projected onto God. We need God's help and healing to begin to learn to trust that God loves us, values us and seeks to bless us.

Question 6. Invite group members to share what has helped them personally. Practices might include meditating on Scriptures such as these and writing daily gratitude lists.

Question 7. Jesus' call to let go of anxieties and to embrace God's kingdom and God's righteousness is a call to a life lived in reliance on and surrender to our Maker. Again, our fears and anxieties often lead to attempts to control what we cannot control, which leaves us resentful, despairing and even more anxious. In addition, our fears and anxieties often cause us to become highly self-focused and self-serving. The life Jesus calls us to is, instead, a life in which we rely on God's loving provision, entrusting ourselves and our wills to God's care. This opens us to experience God's care and frees us to live a life of active love for others.

Question 8. Jesus states clearly that it is God's desire to provide for us and to respond to our requests in generous and loving ways. He points out the way his listeners respond as parents to their children—wanting to give good gifts to their children, wanting to respond to their children's needs. And then he reminds us that God, who, unlike us, is pure love, responds to our needs with love and care that is far beyond what a human parent can imagine.

Question 9. Encourage group members to describe the contrast they see between these two images of God.

Question 10. Help the group explore and reflect on the significance of who God is in ways that are specific and personal. The extent that we are able to trust that we are seen, known and valued by God is the extent we will be able to entrust ourselves to God's care and provision. Many people believe that they are alone in their struggle to trust, but most of us struggle with this, even people who have been following Jesus for many years.

Question 11. That we are to ask, seek and knock is a major theme in Scripture (see, e.g., Lk 11:9, Acts 17:27; Heb 11:6; Jas 1:5). It is not the case that God withholds when we do not ask; God continually pours out sustaining grace and blessing into our lives. But our asking, seeking, knocking is vital because it involves us in a process of (1) realizing that there are things we cannot do on our own, (2) experiencing our need and desires, (3) engaging in relationship with God, (4) experiencing God's specific, personal responses to us, and (5) learning to trust more fully that we are known and loved.

Question 12. As you lead the group in this time of prayer, give members some time to sit quietly with open hands, releasing the things that they are anxious about. Then give them time to sit with open hands to receive from God whatever God might have for them at the moment. Invite the group to share whatever they might want to share about this time of prayer.

Study 8. The God Who Is Weak Versus the God Who Is All-Powerful. Luke 8:22-56.

Purpose: To see God as all-powerful and to trust more fully that God's power is a power that protects, heals and restores us.

Question 1. The text for this study is long. This question will help give the group an overview.

Questions 2, 3, 4 and 5. These moments were clearly stunning to the people who observed them. They knew something supernatural had taken place. Responses to such power can be anything from awe to fear, and encountering the power of such love can be life-changing.

Question 6. Take the time to facilitate this engagement with the passage. Encourage group members to imaginatively enter the scene of each story as a participatory observer as much as they are able. Read the passage out loud as the question indicates—slowly, and with a brief pause after each story. Then allow for three to five minutes of silence to help people enter the passage more deeply. Break the silence by inviting the group to share some of what they experienced and noticed by engaging with these narratives.

Question 9. These stories from Luke show us a God who is with us in ways that are personal, intimate, tender and stunningly powerful. The disciples' fear was responded to and the storm was stilled. The man who was chained and demon-possessed was completely restored. The woman who had suffered for twelve years from an ailment that left her "unclean" was able to touch Jesus, be seen by Jesus and be fully healed. And, in a private moment with a girl's traumatized parents, Jesus touches and speaks and the spirit returns to the child. In every case, Jesus demonstrated God's mighty power and revealed that this is a power that is loving, healing, freeing, compassionate and responsive to our needs.

Question 10. Encourage the group to explore this contrast.

Question 11. Help group members explore the personal significance of these amazing stories of the power of God's love as shown to us in Jesus.

Dale Ryan is CEO of Christian Recovery International. He is also an associate professor of recovery ministry and director of the Fuller Institute for Recovery Ministry at Fuller Theological Seminary. He has consulted with ministries in several countries that are seeking to develop support groups for alcoholics and addicts and their families. Juanita Ryan is a clinical nurse specialist with an M.S.N. in psychiatric mental health nursing, which she has taught at Bethel University, Rio Hondo Community College and Biola University. She is currently a therapist in private practice at Brea Family Counseling Center in Brea, California. Together Dale and Juanita have coauthored The Twelve Steps: A Spiritual Kindergarten, Rooted in God's Love *and* Soul Repair *(coauthored with Jeff VanVonderen), as well as many other Bible study guides.*

What should we study next?

We have LifeGuides for . . .

Knowing Jesus
Advent of the Savior
Following Jesus
I Am
Abiding in Christ
Jesus' Final Week

Knowing God
Meeting God
God's Comfort
God's Love
The 23rd Psalm
Miracles

Growing in the Spirit
Meeting the Spirit
Fruit of the Spirit
Spiritual Gifts
Spiritual Warfare

Looking at the Trinity
Images of Christ
Images of God
Images of the Spirit

Developing Disciplines
Christian Disciplines
God's Word
Hospitality
The Lord's Prayer
Prayer
Praying the Psalms
Sabbath
Worship

Deepening Your Doctrine
Angels
Christian Beliefs
The Cross
End Times
Good & Evil
Heaven
The Kingdom of God
The Story of Scripture

Seekers
Encountering Jesus
Jesus the Reason
Meeting Jesus

Leaders
Christian Leadership
Integrity
Elijah
Joseph

Shaping Your Character
Christian Character
Decisions
Self-Esteem
Parables
Pleasing God
Woman of God
Women of the New Testament
Women of the Old Testament

Living Fully at Every Stage
Singleness
Marriage
Parenting
Couples of the Old Testament
Couples of the New Testament
Growing Older & Wiser

Reaching Our World
Missions
Evangelism
Four Great Loves
Loving Justice

Living Your Faith
Christian Virtues
Forgiveness

Growing in Relationships
Christian Community
Friendship